Marie Antoinette and the truths about France's Doomed

queen

1755-1793

Picture of Maria Teresa

Marie antoinette's mother, Empress of Austria (1717-1780)

Marie Antoinette was a royal Austrian duchess who had married the future French king as part of an alliance between France and Austria. Maria Teresa, the Empress of Austria, forged the alliance as an attempt for both countries to being allies as well as Maria Teresa's personal goal of having some indirect influence on France 's political situation to help Austria become more powerful. Unfortunately The destiny of the marriage partnership turned to be a doomed one as both princes ended up losing their heads to the guillotine in 1793.

Start From the beginning 1770 When Marie went to France to marry the future Louis xvi. This undertaking, initiated by Maria Teresa, was for Marie to marry the dauphin, become queen of France and remain a monarch for the rest of her life. This partnership was part of a renewed alliance between France and Austria, who had been enemies in the past but after the seven years' war and the diplomatic revolution of 1756. France and Austria decided to become partners in a cat and fight strategy war with Britain and Prussia, The partnership between Britain and Prussia would be sealed with a marriage. So on May 16, 1770 .Maria Antonia Josepha Johanna married Louis Auguste at the Palace of Versailles

The royal couple getting married.

The marriage and the crown have led to some interesting observations. It led Marie to being a tragic yet unpopular queen due to her reported extravagances and unpopularity from the French press. It also led Marie to becoming tarnished and the infamous quote “let them eat cake “being attributed to her.

The legacy of Marie Antoinette led to her to becoming one of the most hated queens in history. However there are some truths and other revelations about the last queen of France

1. Marie Antoinette and Louis XVI were not in love with each other but were together for royal duty only.

This is one big reason the couple did not have any children for seven years. Marie Antoinette first thought Louis was clumsy, and not someone who was attractive. She was interested in sex but

Louis, on the other hand, was not interested in sex, he was interested in eating and going hunting. These two were together because of state only. They did become loyal to one another and became best friends. These guys were complete opposite from one another .Maybe the other reason why they did not have sex, for seven years was because they were children

In the 21 st century, a couple getting married at 14, 0r 15 years old would be considered illegal in the United States and many advanced countries due to the age. Being a fourteen year old is considered a child nowadays. A lot of fourteen year old children do not have sex at this age. I would guess that Marie Antoinette and Louis

XVI were in ,essence ,children and 200 years ago, many people in France thought that fourteen or fifteen years of age in a royal household was ripe for marriage because they thought this age was an adult age.

2. **Marie Antoinette was a cruel woman who did not care for her subjects.**

Marie Antoinette was extravagant and this was induced by her royal background. She was somewhat callous due to the financial crisis in her country and her willingness to continue to spend, and buy things for herself but she was generous at times. She had sometimes given money to some charities in Paris. She had allowed some peasant adults and children to live at Versailles. . She also made an quote regarding the France bread shortages, and the poor in 1775. **It is quite certain that in seeing the people who treat we so well despite their own misfortune, we are more obliged than ever to work hard for their happiness. The King seems to understand this truth.**[9]

3. **a lot of allegations made by the French press about Marie Antoinette were not true regarding her having lots of lovers.**

Marie Antoinette did not have a lot of lovers, and did not intended to hurt the poor people economically in her country .She was very conservative , by nature, but she may have had one extra-marital relationship with a Swedish count named Axel Fersen.

4. Marie did not say let them eat cake

The queen did not say "let them eat cake" but this was attributed to her because of her bad reputation caused by the French press as well as her initial unwillingness to respond to the savage attacks that ultimately led to her being guillotine in 1793.

Pictures of her homes at versalles, The petit trianon and the hameau de reine.

Versailles queens apartment

The petit trianon

The hameau de la reine

Marie being guillotined oct 16,1793 in Paris at the place de La revolution

Marie’s gravesite at Saint Denis Basilica in Paris France

MARIE-ANTOINETTE
D'AUTRICHE
REINE DE FRANCE
ET DE NAVARRE
1755 - 1793

www.ingramcontent.com/pod-product-compliance
Ingram Content Group UK Ltd.
Pitfield, Milton Keynes, MK11 3LW, UK
UKHW041902190726
13854UKWH00003B/1042